ILLUSTRATION BY JASON KARAS AND ERIC MILLIKIN

This illustration was built from more than 1,000 photos sent to the Free Press by Detroit fans from all over the world.

T0095954

THE ROSTER

EDITOR
Ryan Ford

ASSISTANT EDITORS
Mari delaGarza
Shelly Solon Darby

PHOTO EDITOR
Diane Weiss

DESIGNERS
Ryan Ford
Jeff Tarsha

PROJECT COORDINATOR
Steve Dorsey

COPY EDITORS
David Darby
Tim Marcinkoski

GRAPHICS TECHNICIANS
Chuck Whitman
Erin Fuhs

COVER PHOTO
Diane Weiss

COVER DESIGN
Ryan Ford

SPORTS EDITOR
Gene Myers

SPECIAL THANKS
Mitch Albom,
Elisha Anderson,
Jo-Ann Barnas,
Anthony Fenech,
A.J. Hartley,
Nancy Laughlin,
John Lowe,
Drew Sharp,
Ric Simon,
George Sipple,
Shawn Windsor,
and the Anchor Bar

AVAILABLE FROM THE FREE PRESS BOOKSTORE

THE ULTIMATE TIGERS LIBRARY!

TO ORDER ANY OF THESE TITLES OR OTHER GEAR, GO TO FREEP.COM/ BOOKSTORE OR CALL 800-245-5082

THE TEAM!
ROAR RESTORED
Relive the Tigers' magical return to glory in 2006. From Jim Leyland's hiring to the emergence of Justin Verlander as a star to electric victories over the Yankees and A's in the playoffs, it all led to Detroit's first World Series since 1984.

THE BROADCASTING!
ERNIE: OUR VOICE OF SUMMER
Reflect on Ernie Harwell's long career as the acclaimed voice of the Detroit Tigers in 128 pages of rich, historic photos and defining quotes by and about Detroit's very own Voice of Summer.

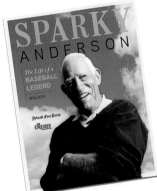

THE MANAGER!
SPARKY ANDERSON: THE LIFE OF A BASEBALL LEGEND
Celebrate the life and times of Sparky Anderson in this hardcover book. We reflect on his long career in 128 full-color pages of historic photos about a good-field, no-hit middle infielder from South Dakota who became a managing legend.

OTHER FREE PRESS TIGERS BOOKS
- Century of Champions
- Ernie Harwell: Stories from my life in baseball
- Ernie Harwell: Life after baseball
- Ernie Harwell: Breaking 90
- Ernie Harwell: Extra innings with the voice of summer
- The Corner
- Corner to CoPa

Detroit Free Press

TRIUMPH BOOKS

615 W. Lafayette Blvd.
Detroit MI, 48226
©2012 by Detroit Free Press. All rights reserved

Published by Triumph Books

No part of this book may be reproduced or transmitted in any form or by any means, electronic or mechanical, including photocopying, recording or by an informantion storage system, without the permission of the publisher, except where permitted by law.

DAYS OF ROAR!

THE TIGERS' UNFORGETTABLE 2012 SEASON AND MIGUEL CABRERA'S TRIPLE CROWN

crown 'em!

MIGUEL CABRERA – AT THE PLATE AND IN THE FIELD – TRIUMPHANTLY LED THE TIGERS TO A HISTORIC SEASON

O h, this season had moments. Amazing moments and achievements.

There was the thrilling, dramatic pennant race.

And that unforgettable night in Kansas City when Miguel Cabrera won the Triple Crown — among one of the top 10 greatest sports achievements in Detroit sports history.

And the kiss — Al Alburquerque's full-lipped smooch of a baseball that ticked off the Oakland Athletics.

And that wild scene in the Tigers' clubhouse as they celebrated going to the World Series.

But let's back up and take this slowly. Let's savor it.

Let's go back to the first scene. The one that set up everything. The one that gave us a small hint of what was to come.

Miguel Cabrera and Prince Fielder walked out of the Tigers' clubhouse in Lakeland, Fla., and came down the sidewalk walking side by side.

JEFF SEIDEL REFLECTS ON DETROIT'S WILD RIDE FROM SPRING TRAINING TO THE WORLD SERIES

"Look who we got!" Cabrera screamed, to a group of fans. "Look who we got!"

Cabrera had the excited, wide-eyed expression of a child who had just opened a present.

Look who we got!

Cabrera and Fielder went to a back field and took batting practice, smashing home runs high into the trees. That is how it started, on a warm, glorious day at spring training.

From the start, Fielder and Cabrera had a bond. They knew how they could help each other. One protecting the other. One pushing the other.

That is what led to their wild handshake.

And the chase for the Triple Crown.

And race for the American League pennant.

And the sprint into the World Series.

This is how it started. On a warm day in Lakeland.

The roars would come later.

CONTINUED ON NEXT PAGE >>

Crown jewel

Miguel Cabrera's daughter ran up to see her dad receive a mock crown from Frank Robinson as Cabrera was selected the Hank Aaron Award winner for most outstanding player in the American League. Aaron said of the Triple Crown: "It is something that you are blessed with."

MANDI WRIGHT

Twice as great

Former Tiger and Hall of Famer Al Kaline posed for a picture with 2011 American League MVP Justin Verlander at Comerica Park before Game 3 of the World Series. Kaline was part of the Tigers' world championship team in 1968.

<< CONTINUED FROM PREVIOUS PAGE

THERE WAS NO GIVING UP

This was a team that never game up fighting.

The Tigers were six games behind the Chicago White Sox on June 12, but didn't give up. They were three games back with just 15 to play.

But they didn't give up. They kept fighting — two steps forward and one step back — and the White Sox started to fall apart.

And then, suddenly — look at that! — they were in first.

Which brings us to another moment. It was a late September afternoon, and Doug Fister was on the mound against the Royals.

Fister struck out nine straight batters, setting an American League record, and he had no idea why everybody was freaking out.

"Go in there, the guys will tell you," Fielder said.

It was an amazing, historic accomplishment.

Especially for a guy not known for his strikeouts.

IT TOOK TIME TO FIND THE RIGHT MIX

Oh, sure, this team had flaws.

Tigers president and GM Dave Dombrowski tried to fix them midseason, bringing in Omar Infante to play second base and Anibal Sanchez to be the team's fourth starter.

Dombrowski kept tinkering with the roster, pulling players up from the minors, bringing in players and discarding them.

And in the end, this team had something that worked, a low-key mix of superstars and role players.

There was Justin Verlander, the reigning MVP and Cy Young Award winner. Verlander had a quiet year — for him. He had some ups, some downs. But when it was all done, when you looked back on his numbers — a 17-8 record, a 2.64 earned-run average and an American League-leading 239 strikeouts — he was spectacular, once again.

Verlander pitched a four-hit shutout to win Game 5 of the AL Division Series against the A's. And the Tigers swept the Yankees and went to the World Series. And yes, the Giants

CONTINUED ON NEXT PAGE >>

Nice work

Jim Leyland gave Prince Fielder a fist bump as they talked during batting practice before a game against Oakland in the division series. Leyland said early in the season: "I'm starting to get to know him a little bit, but I can see almost the best way to keep him going is to pretty much leave him alone. He knows what he needs to do."

JULIAN H. GONZALEZ

JULIAN H. GONZALEZ

Hitting it off

Big bats Prince Fielder and Miguel Cabrera became fast friends in their first year as teammates soon after arriving at spring training. Fielder was in awe of his friend's talent. "I don't think he truly understands how great of a player he really is," Fielder said.

<< CONTINUED FROM PREVIOUS PAGE

kicked the Tigers' butts. The Giants deserved to win the World Series.

Which means that years from now, when the historians look back at this team, this season will be remembered for the Triple Crown.

CABRERA WAS THE ONE CONSTANT

Which brings us to the final moment.

A small moment that said everything about Cabrera.

It was in the middle of the pennant race. In the middle of his chase for the Triple Crown. And Cabrera went out to take batting practice, and he spotted Prince Fielder's two sons. They ran up to him, "Miggy! Miggy!"

Cabrera performed a handshake with the boys, the same silly handshake he did with Prince Fielder after home runs, big plays and victories. Hand slaps. Front. Back. Silly gestures. Lots of smiles. End with a hug.

As he waited to take his turn in the batting cage, Cabrera hit the boys soft, easy pop-ups on the grass behind home plate, and then, 5-year-old Gage Brookens joined the group. His grandfather is Tom Brookens, the first-base coach.

"I got it, I got it," they screamed, trying to catch the ball, their gloves stabbing into the air.

Cabrera broke into a giant smile.

At one point, Gage Brookens got hurt, colliding with one of Fielder's sons. Cabrera walked over to the boys and took a knee — right there in the middle of batting practice. Comforting Gage. Making sure he was OK.

Seriously. There was the best hitter in baseball, tending to a banged-up kid, in the middle of a pennant race. In the middle of a quest to win a Triple Crown.

On his way to the World Series.

And he was playing with some kids.

That is the essence of Miguel Cabrera. Loose. Fun-loving. Just an overgrown kid, who became the first Triple Crown winner in 45 years.

What a wild, unforgettable ride.

DAYS OF ROAR

7

HEAD OF HIS CLASS

MOVE OVER, ECK! JV BECOMES THE FIRST PITCHER SINCE 1992 TO WIN THE CY YOUNG AND MVP IN THE SAME SEASON

Elite pitcher

On Nov. 21, 2011, Justin Verlander became just the 10th pitcher — but third Tiger — to win the Cy Young and MVP in the same season. The right-hander received 13 first-place votes for the MVP award and finished well ahead of the Red Sox's Jacoby Ellsbury. He was a unanimous choice for the Cy Young Award. The last pitcher to win the Cy Young and MVP in the same season was Oakland's Dennis Eckersley in 1992.

ROBERT HANASHIRO/USA TODAY

HONOR SOCIETY

Right-hander Justin Verlander became just the 10th pitcher, and the third Tiger, to win the Cy Young and MVP in the same season since 1956. Denny McLain pulled off the double in 1968 and Guillermo (Willie) Hernandez in 1984. The list:

1958
DON NEWCOMBE
Dodgers

1963
SANDY KOUFAX
Dodgers

1968
BOB GIBSON
Cardinals

1968
DENNY McLAIN
Tigers

1971
VIDA BLUE
Athletics

1981
ROLLIE FINGERS
Brewers

1984
GUILLERMO HERNANDEZ
Tigers

1986
ROGER CLEMENS
Red Sox

1992
DENNIS ECKERSLEY
Athletics

2011
JUSTIN VERLANDER
Tigers

Detroit Free Press

VERLANDER

2011
MVP
AMERICAN LEAGUE'S MOST VALUABLE PLAYER

RICK NEASE

A few reasons to be proud

In Justin Verlander's Cy Young and MVP season, he went 24-5 with a 2.40 ERA and 250 strikeouts (tops in the league). "This is the latest pinch-me moment," his father, Richard Verlander, said after learning that Justin had won the MVP award. "I think the thing we're most proud of is that Justin has stayed true to his roots. He's still the same kid from Goochland (Va.)."

JULIAN H. GONZALEZ

JULIAN H. GONZALEZ

No resting on his laurels

Justin Verlander answered questions from fans during a Tigers winter caravan stop at the Palladium 12 Theatre in Birmingham. During another stop, he said of his awards: "It's not something I'm going to think about, dwell on. It's not like I had one great year. ... I'm going to continue to push forward and basically do the same thing I've been doing since I got here, and that's to try and improve year to year."

DIANE WEISS

A star is sidelined

In 2011, Victor Martinez had 103 RBIs, 40 doubles, 12 home runs and a .330 batting average as the Tigers' primary designated hitter. The Tigers suffered a major off-season blow when he had a season-ending knee injury during agility drills in January. Martinez had a torn anterior cruciate ligament and also needed surgery to repair the medial and lateral meniscus in his left knee. "We were dealt a blow — Victor Martinez is an integral part of our club, and we will miss him," Tigers general manager and president Dave Dombrowski said in January. "However, good clubs have to be resilient, and we have a resilient group of guys."

Confident of a comeback

Victor Martinez showed up to the Tigers' spring-training camp in Lakeland, Fla., on crutches after the first of two surgeries to repair his knee. He told the Free Press: "I know I'm going to get back in and keep rolling with the team. I'm not even 1% concerned about it. I'm a guy who always works hard. If this is going to change anything, it's going to make me work even harder."

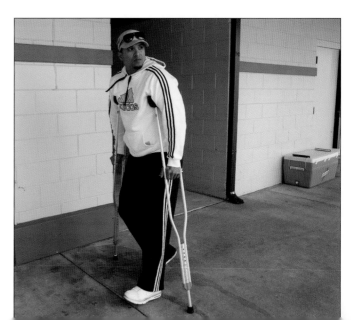

JULIAN H. GONZALEZ

DAYS OF ROAR
12

DOWN FOR THE COUNT

DESIGNATED HITTER'S TORN ACL LEAVES A HOLE IN THE MIDDLE OF 2012 TIGERS LINEUP

A clubhouse leader

An injured Victor Martinez, left, was greeted by Tigers coaches Lloyd McClendon, center, and Rafael Belliard at the team's spring-training camp in March. Tigers pitcher Rick Porcello said in January, "He's very consistent with his leadership. He's always excited. He brings the best out of everybody. It's obviously tough. A guy hits .330 in the middle of your lineup and is a leader in the clubhouse — you never want to lose a guy like that. But it's just a challenge we're going to have to overcome."

JULIAN H. GONZALEZ

BACK IN THE FAMILY

TIGERS SHELL OUT MEGA-BUCKS TO SIGN MEGA-SIZED FIRST BASEMAN WITH DETROIT HISTORY

JULIAN H. GONZALEZ

Prince of Detroit

Prince Fielder whispered to his then-7-year-old son Jadyn after the slugger's news conference on Jan. 26 to introduce the newest Tiger at Comerica Park. The Tigers signed Fielder to the richest contract in club history: a $214-million, nine-year deal. "I don't think there is a baseball bone in my body that doesn't get excited about the move," Tigers general manager Dave Dombrowski said of signing Fielder.

JULIAN H. GONZALEZ

A difference maker

Tigers general manager Dave Dombrowski, left, and owner Mike Ilitch, right, watch left-handed slugger Prince Fielder put on his new jersey. "I said there's some solid guys out there, Mr. I, but there's only one difference maker, and that's Prince Fielder," Dombrowski said of how he sold Fielder as a replacement for Victor Martinez." Fielder was brought in after V-Mart, a designated hitter, was sidelined for the season with a knee injury.

In a different league

Before he was a Tiger, Prince Fielder was with the Milwaukee Brewers for seven seasons. In 2011, he was the All-Star Game MVP after the National League beat the American League, 5-1. Longtime Tigers fans saw Fielder's power long before he joined the Brewers. He is the son of former Tigers slugger Cecil Fielder, and one day at Tiger Stadium in the mid-1990s, a 12-year-old Prince hit a batting-practice home run.

JULIAN H. GONZALEZ

JULIAN H. GONZALEZ

Salesmanship

Sports agent Scott Boras, left, helped work out the deal that brought Prince Fielder to Detroit. Tigers owner Mike Ilitch said Boras "knows everything about the Detroit Tigers. I was flabbergasted. Utility players, everybody. He went through a big discussion and pointed out some of the things he thought were necessary to win a World Series. There's great salesmanship involved with that. But the guy is an encyclopedia when it comes to knowing the teams and knowing the people who are associated with the organizations."

Bankrolling a winning team

Tigers owner Mike Ilitch, right, invested a lot of money in Fielder. "I know this is a lot more money, but I go by my instincts," Ilitch said. "And my instincts tell me this is going to work out fine. I'm not going to worry about it."

JULIAN H. GONZALEZ

A family man

Prince Fielder and his family leave his introductory news conference Jan. 26, 2012. Clockwise from left are Fielder, wife Chanel, and sons Jadyn and Haven. Fielder might never have had the chance to join the Tigers if he hadn't gone on a trip overseas to renew his vows with Chanel. During that vacation, he put on hold his decision on where to sign as a free agent.

JULIAN H. GONZALEZ

the king

A MOVE FROM FIRST TO THIRD BASE DIDN'T SLOW THIS TIGERS SLUGGER FROM WINNING BASEBALL'S FIRST TRIPLE CROWN IN 45 YEARS

Royal triumph

Miguel Cabrera won the Triple Crown for the first time since Boston's Carl Yastrzemski in 1967. He finished the season with a league-leading 44 home runs, 139 RBIs and a .330 batting average.

"All I could think of then was 'Wow, I really did it,'" Cabrera said. "It's just unbelievable. That's the only thing that I could say."

JULIAN H. GONZALEZ

KIRTHMON F. DOZIER

Friends and sluggers

Prince Fielder and Miguel Cabrera celebrated after their four-game sweep of the New York Yankees in the American League Championship Series. After Cabrera won the Triple Crown, Fielder said: "Without him being a team guy and moving to third base, which is not easy, I probably wouldn't be here. I kept thanking him because I'm just so glad that he let me be a part of it. I mean, he's Miguel Cabrera. He doesn't have to change positions to accommodate somebody else because of everything he's done. But he did. And not only did he change positions, but he won the Triple Crown in the year that he does it. Again, how can anyone not look at that and not come away amazed at how great he really is? And the thing is. I don't think he truly understands how great of a player he really is."

Hats off to Cabrera

The batting helmets of Miguel Cabrera (24) and Prince Fielder with postseason logos were side-by-side before the first game of the American League Division Series against the Oakland A's.

JULIAN H. GONZALEZ

Position change

Tigers third baseman Miguel Cabrera gave Prince Fielder's son, Haven, a high five after finishing fielding work during spring training in Lakeland, Fla. Cabrera moved from first to third base to make room for Fielder in the infield.

JULIAN H. GONZALEZ

DIANE WEISS

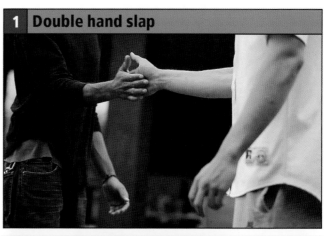

SHAKE ON IT!

Throughout the season, Miguel Cabrera and Prince Fielder shared an elaborate handshake after home runs, big plays and victories.

Well, don't ask Cabrera or Fielder about it. Neither offered much insight into how they came up with the handshake when the Free Press asked about it. They seemed quite pleased with the result of their handy work and that fans seem to enjoy it. But that's about all they would say.

"It's top secret," said Fielder, who declined to walk reporters through the moves that they insisted didn't have a name. "Can't do it."

Fielder, though, said he had been approached randomly by people wanting to do the handshake.

"It definitely is awkward," he said, "when I see grown men wanting to do it when I'm walking down the street."

But is it really that hard? Not if you ask Bo Thomas of Troy, who has been a Tigers fan since he was in diapers. He said he watched their moves on TV, then would rewind and watch again until he learned them and could teach them to others.

"It looks a lot harder than it really is," Thomas said.

Here, Thomas and his friend Jarrett Evans of Auburn Hills demonstrate the seven steps to shake like a Tigers slugger:

2 Reversed, single hand slap

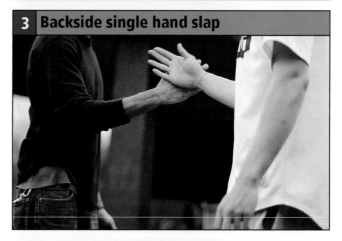

3 Backside single hand slap

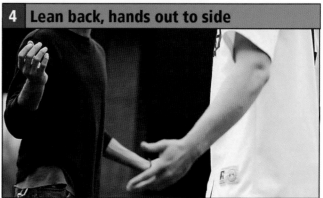

4 Lean back, hands out to side

DIANE WEISS

5 Cabrera sprinkles

7 Bear hug

JARRAD HENDERSON AND DAVID PIERCE

6 Fielder sprinkles

Practice makes perfect

JULIAN H. GONZALEZ

Miguel Cabrera has a hit in every league championship series game in which he has played. That's 17 games with the Tigers and Marlins.

JULIAN H. GONZALEZ

Not grounded

Miguel Cabrera practiced taking grounders at third base during spring training. He had not played third base since 2008. "When you've got superstars that are cooperative, that's just a big bonus for the manager and the coaching staff," Tigers manager Jim Leyland said during spring training.

Who's on third?

Miguel Cabrera had to work on his fielding during spring training after being moved from first to third base. He showed up at the training complex at Lakeland, Fla., noticeably trimmer than he was in 2011 and ready to try hard. "We have to work hard and see what happens," he said during spring training. "I think we can control that — work hard, try to do the best we can and see what we can do."

JULIAN H. GONZALEZ

Field of dreams

Miguel Cabrera was third with a .966 fielding percentage among everyday American League third basemen.

KIRTHMON F. DOZIER

Another milestone

After hitting his 299th career home run in the first inning off Chicago White Sox right-hander Philip Humber, Miguel Cabrera hit No. 300 in the third inning on July 22.

JULIAN H. GONZALEZ

JULIAN H. GONZALEZ

Mr. 300

Miguel Cabrera's milestone blast gave the Tigers a 4-1 lead in the third inning against their division rivals. The ball went into the camera well in centerfield — for an estimated 457-foot home run that made him just the 14th person in baseball history to reach 300 homers before age 30. The Tigers won the game, 6-4.

DIANE WEISS

A Tiger, through and through

Never putting himself first, Miguel Cabrera was a true team player. "I'm just so happy to be a part of this team," he said after winning the Triple Crown. "(The Triple Crown) belongs to them as much as me. I don't do it without them."

But also, he's Batman

Miguel Cabrera hit 40 doubles during the 2012 regular season and a career-high 48 in 2011.

MANDI WRIGHT

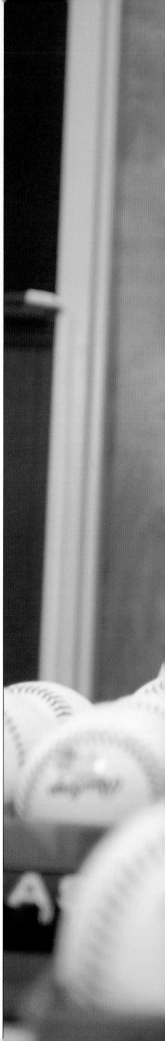

Please sign here

Miguel Cabrera autographed baseballs for the players' association during the Tigers' 2012 photo day at their spring training complex at Lakeland, Fla.

JULIAN H. GONZALEZ

A Detroit state of mind

Tim Delcavo, left, of Orlando held up a banner of Miguel Cabrera with his father, Tony Delcavo, of Castle Rock, Colo., before the Tigers faced the Oakland Athletics in Game 1 of the American League Division Series at Comerica Park. Tony Delcavo, who was brought up in Connecticut, decided he wanted to be a Tigers fan and not a Yankees fan in 1955. "I wanted to be different," Tony Delcavo said.

MANDI WRIGHT

Fan-tastic

Before Game 3 of the American League Division Series at Oakland, from left, Laura Vasher of Las Vegas, and G.G. Gunther and Vanessa Lee, both of San Francisco, wore crowns in honor of Miguel Cabrera's Triple Crown win.

JULIAN H. GONZALEZ

A royal welcome in Kansas City

Fans dressed up to honor Miguel Cabrera's Triple Crown achievement during the last game of the regular season at Kansas City.

JULIAN H. GONZALEZ

CROWNING GLORY

Miguel Cabrera's Triple Crown, that is, leading his league in home runs, runs batted in and batting average, is the 17th in baseball history, and the first since 1967. The list:

1878
PAUL HINES
Providence (NL)
HR: 4
RBI: 50
AVERAGE: .358

1887
TIP O'NEILL
St. Louis (AA)
HR: 14
RBI: 123
AVERAGE: .435

1901
NAP LAJOIE
Philadelphia (AL)
HR: 14
RBI: 125
AVERAGE: .426

1909
TY COBB
Detroit (AL)
HR: 9
RBI: 107
AVERAGE: .377

1922
ROGERS HORNSBY
St. Louis (NL)
HR: 42
RBI: 152
AVERAGE: .401

1925
ROGERS HORNSBY
St. Louis (NL)
HR: 39
RBI: 143
AVERAGE: .403

1932
JIMMIE FOXX
Philadelphia (AL)
HR: 58
RBI: 169
AVERAGE: .364

1933
CHUCK KLEIN
Philadelphia (NL)
HR: 28
RBI: 120
AVERAGE: .368

1933
JIMMIE FOXX
Philadelphia (AL)
HR: 48
RBI: 163
AVERAGE: .356

1934
LOU GEHRIG
New York (AL)
HR: 49
RBI: 165
AVERAGE: .363

1937
JOE MEDWICK
St. Louis (NL)
HR: 31
RBI: 154
AVERAGE: .374

1942
TED WILLIAMS
Boston (AL)
HR: 36
RBI: 137
AVERAGE: .356

1947
TED WILLIAMS
Boston (AL)
HR: 32
RBI: 114
AVERAGE: .343

1956
MICKEY MANTLE
New York (AL)
HR: 52
RBI: 130
AVERAGE: .353

1966
FRANK ROBINSON
Baltimore (AL)
HR: 49
RBI: 122
AVERAGE: .316

1967
CARL YASTRZEMSKI
Boston (AL)
HR: 44
RBI: 121
AVERAGE: .326

"This is an incredible accomplishment for a gifted young man, and Miguel should be proud of his all-around excellence and consistency throughout the season."

FRANK ROBINSON, 1966 TRIPLE CROWN WINNER

2012
MIGUEL CABRERA
Detroit (AL)
HR: 44
RBI: 139
AVERAGE: .330

2012
TRIPLE CROWN
MIGUEL
CABRERA

''It was great that I could share it with my team-mates.''

Home Runs
44

Batting Average
.330

RBIs
139

Detroit Free Press

PHOTOS: DENNY MEDLEY, PETER G. AIKEN/US PRESSWIRE, ED ZURGA/GETTY IMAGES

RICK NEASE

POSTER DESIGN: RICK NEASE/DETROIT FREE PRESS

Double trouble

Miguel Cabrera led the American League in batting two years in a row — with a .344 average in 2011 and .330 in 2012.

KIRTHMON F. DOZIER

DIANE WEISS

Under the lights

Miguel Cabrera almost always gave the fans at night games a treat when the lights came one: The third baseman hit an astounding .354 in night games in 2012, with 23 homers.

All-Star lineup

Justin Verlander, Prince Fielder and Miguel Cabrera made the American League All-Star team. It was Cabrera's seventh time being selected to the All-Star Game. Cabrera said he enjoys the rest during the All-Star break but he also enjoys the chance to play with the game's best. "It's a good time," he said.

JULIAN H. GONZALEZ

Celebrating good times

Miguel Cabrera briefly joined in the champagne celebration in the locker room at Kansas City on Oct. 1, after the Tigers won the American League Central. His teammates chanted "M-V-P, M-V-P, M-V-P."

JULIAN H. GONZALEZ

A Central title

Miguel Cabrera celebrated with manager Jim Leyland after defeating Kansas City, 6-3, on Oct. 1 to win the American League Central. Cabrera went 4-for-5 in that game and hit a solo home run in the sixth inning.

JULIAN H. GONZALEZ

JULIAN H. GONZALEZ

September heat

A Tigers fan held an MVP sign as Miguel Cabrera came to bat on Sept. 18. Cabrera was hot in September (27 RBIs, 10 home runs and a .308 batting average) as the Tigers surged to overtake the Chicago White Sox to win the American League Central.

ERIC SEALS

Yankee chiller

Miguel Cabrera hit a two-run home run in the fourth inning to give the Tigers a 4-0 lead in Game 4 of the American League Championship Series. The Tigers beat the New York Yankees, 8-1, at Comerica Park to complete the four-game sweep.

Postseason magic

Miguel Cabrera went 5-for-16 with four RBIs and a .313 batting average in the Tigers' American League Championship Series sweep of the New York Yankees. "We did it!" Cabrera hollered after the Tigers took the best-of-seven series.

JULIAN H. GONZALEZ

Paper Tiger

A cutout paper version of Miguel Cabrera — complete with the shades — had its photo taken around the old train station in downtown Detroit.

SUSAN TUSA

DIANE WEISS

Down the stretch

Miguel Cabrera got help stretching before a game late in the season. "He's a great hitter having a great year. He played his best when we needed him to, down the stretch," teammate Justin Verlander told the Sporting News as it named Cabrera its player of the year.

JULIAN H. GONZALEZ

For laughs

Comedian George Lopez, in town for a show, stopped by to see Miguel Cabrera and the Tigers during the weekend before the World Series. "I told him a Latino winning the Triple Crown is as impressive as having a black president, or potentially an orange one, " Lopez said.

Teammates and countrymen

Miguel Cabrera hugged former Tigers outfielder Magglio Ordoñez at the retirement ceremony for Ordoñez this summer at Comerica Park. Both sluggers are Venezuelan.

JULIAN H. GONZALEZ

Down for the count

Miguel Cabrera struck out to end a 1-2-3 eighth inning for Giants starter-turned-reliever Tim Lincecum in Game 1 of the World Series. Cabrera had one hit in the game, an RBI single in the sixth, the Tigers' only run until they added two in the ninth.

JULIAN H. GONZALEZ

A family affair

Miguel Cabrera's family was on hand as he received his Triple Crown honor before Game 3 of the World Series at Comerica Park as was commissioner Bud Selig. He said of Cabrera: "He's had a truly remarkable offensive season, winning the first Triple Crown since 1967, ending the longest gap between winning Triple Crowns. He now stands amongst an elite group of the game's legends."

MANDI WRIGHT

King Cabrera

A Tigers fan holds up a sign honoring Miguel Cabrera and his Triple Crown at Comerica Park before the opening game of the ALDS against Oakland.

KIRTHMON F. DOZIER

MANDI WRIGHT

Making the play

Miguel Cabrera showed he was more than just a big bat as here he threw to first, retiring the Giants' Hunter Pence in Game 3 of the World Series. Cabrera switched to third base this season after previously playing first for the Tigers.

the ace

FROM VIDEO GAMES TO NEAR-PERFECT GAMES, THE LANKY RIGHTY WAS SEEMINGLY EVERYWHERE IN 2012

Still must-see JV

Justin Verlander followed up his Cy Young and MVP season by leading the league in strikeouts with 239. He went 17-8 with a 2.64 ERA in 2012 and pitched six complete games to lead the American League.

DERRICK HINGLE/U.S. PRESSWIRE

JULIAN H. GONZALEZ

A laughing matter?

Justin Verlander kept it light during spring training. "The worst thing I can do is put more pressure on me based on what happened last season," he said. "That's why I don't focus on numbers like everybody else. I'm working on becoming a better pitcher, and I know I can accomplish that even if the actual numbers might not jump out at everybody like last year."

The need for speed

Justin Verlander was the starting pitcher for the American League in the All-Star Game. Since the game was a showcase, he threw uncharacteristic early fire, touching 100 m.p.h. several times in his one inning. He gave up five earned runs and two walks.

DAYS OF ROAR
50

PETER G. AIKEN/USA TODAY

Dominating the AL

Justin Verlander went 3-0 in the American League Division Series and AL Championship Series combined. He allowed just two hits and had a 0.74 ERA in those series while striking out 25.

JULIAN H. GONZALEZ

Former teammates

Justin Verlander, right, talked with former Tiger Carlos Guillen before Guillen was inducted into the Hispanic Heritage Baseball Hall of Fame on Aug. 4 at Comerica Park. Guillen and Verlander played together in 2005-11.

DIANE WEISS

DAYS OF ROAR
51

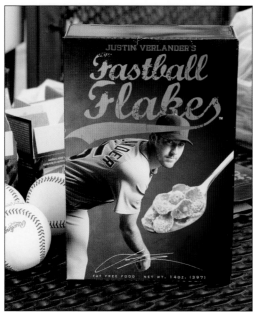

JULIAN H. GONZALEZ

Marketable man

"Fastball Flakes" hit the shelves before the Tigers hit 2012 spring training. They were sold exclusively at Detroit-area Meijer stores.

DIANE WEISS

Brothers in arms

Tigers pitcher Justin Verlander hung out with his brother, Ben Verlander, at batting practice before a game against the Baltimore Orioles on Aug. 18 at Comerica Park. Ben Verlander was a baseball player at Old Dominion, Justin's alma mater.

First in the rotation

A Tigers fan held up a giant Justin Verlander head during the opening ceremonies of the American League Division Series against the Oakland Athletics on Oct. 6, 2012. Verlander allowed just three hits and one run over seven innings in the Tigers' playoff-opening victory.

KIRTHMON F. DOZIER

JULIAN H. GONZALEZ

Collecting K's

Tigers fans held up 14 K's for Justin Verlander's strikeouts to end the eighth inning of his 7-2 victory over the New York Yankees on Aug. 6 at Comerica Park. His 130th pitch of the night was 100 m.p.h. and the Tigers got their fifth straight victory.

He's not sitting down on the job

Justin Verlander got in this fielding drill during spring training in Lakeland, Fla.

JULIAN H. GONZALEZ

One-hit wonder

Justin Verlander flirted with what could have been his third career no-hitter on May 18 against the Pittsburgh Pirates. He left to a standing ovation from the 41,661 at Comerica Park after striking out 12 in a complete-game one-hitter that the Tigers won, 6-0.

JULIAN H. GONZALEZ

KIRTHMON F. DOZIER

A bonding experience

"You go through 162 games with what's like your family," Justin Verlander said before he started Game 1 of the American League Division Series against Oakland. "I think that's what makes it so special to get into baseball, in particular, because of the number of games and what you go through in a series."

Picture perfect

New Tiger Prince Fielder, who signed with Detroit in the off-season, posed on team photo day in February at Lakeland, Fla.

In the spring-training opener, Fielder received a big hand from the crowd at Joker Marchant Stadium.

After the game, the new first baseman said of being in camp with Detroit: "I'm in a dream right now, having a great time. It's pretty cool. Everything worked out great. I'm ecstatic."

JULIAN H. GONZALEZ

the prince

FROM DAY 1, THIS
$214-MILLION MAN WAS
A PERFECT FIT IN THE
MIDDLE OF THE TIGERS'
CLUBHOUSE AND THE
MIDDLE OF THE
TIGERS' LINEUP

KIRTHMON F. DOZIER

A happy meeting

Manager Jim Leyland and Prince Fielder hugged after the Game 4 victory against the Yankees at Comerica Park. The win clinched Detroit's four-game sweep in the American League Championship Series. Fielder is a quiet leader for the Tigers, and Leyland is OK with that: "He comes out to beat the other team, comes out to play, comes out to do his job – and goes home."

A fan favorite

Prince Fielder was all smiles as he took time out for a photo with a group of Alpha Kappa Alpha sorority sisters before a Tigers game in April at Comerica Park.

Fielder certainly doesn't seem shy with fans. The Free Press received photos from fans with whom he stopped to take photos at spring training in Lakeland all season long.

KIRTHMON F. DOZIER

Sunny skies

Prince Fielder was excited to be with the Tigers in spring training at Lakeland, Fla. He was looking forward to wearing the Old English D for the first time in the regular season. "I think I will appreciate it even more once the season starts and I see how those fans get excited," he said at the first spring-training game.

JULIAN H. GONZALEZ

STEVEN R. NICKERSON

From boy to a man

Prince Fielder was in Lakeland as a 9-year-old in 1994 with his dad, Cecil, who played for the Tigers for six seasons before being traded to the Yankees in 1996. Prince was happy to finally wear the Old English D as a player in 2012. "As a kid, I was wearing it a lot," Fielder said this spring.

At home in Detroit

Prince Fielder is now a fixture in Detroit, thanks to his nine-year, $214-million deal. He fit in right away as a newcomer. Plus, Detroiters knew Prince as a boy when his father played here.

He said on Opening Day: "The fans made me feel real comfortable."

Smooth slide

After having spent his whole career in the National League with the Brewers, some wondered if Prince Fielder would have trouble adjusting to the AL. He didn't: "It's not that big a challenge, at least not for me." He said of joining a new team: "It's just like going to a new school. After you meet the guys, after a couple of days, you get comfortable."

DIANE WEISS

JULIAN H. GONZALEZ

Big bat

Prince Fielder provided the Tigers with more power, and maybe even more important, he forced opponents to pitch to Triple Crown winner Miguel Cabrera.

Fielder finished the regular season hitting .313 with a .412 on-base percentage and drove in 108 runs. And he played in all 162 games.

JULIAN H. GONZALEZ

JULIAN H. GONZALEZ

Watch and learn

Prince Fielder dropped his bat, knowing this one is going out of the park for a three-run home run. He hit 30 home runs in the regular season for the Tigers. Perhaps Fielder's most impressive home-run display was in July in Kansas City when he blasted the competition in the All-Star Game Home Run Derby to take the crown.

Great catch

New first baseman Prince Fielder just made this catch on a throw from third baseman Miguel Cabrera, the Tigers' former first baseman. Fielder remained grateful for Cabrera's sacrifice: "He doesn't have to change positions to accommodate somebody else because of everything he's done."

JULIAN H. GONZALEZ

DIANE WEISS

New York state of mind

Prince Fielder waited for a pickoff throw, trying to get the Yankees' Ichiro Suzuki out at first. He didn't, but it didn't matter in the outcome of Game 2 of the ALCS. The Tigers had the Yankees' number even if Fielder's numbers weren't great. He went 4-for-17 in the series.

Highs and lows

Prince Fielder let out a yell after sliding safely into second base during the ninth inning of a game down the stretch. The Tigers experienced plenty of up and downs, as did Fielder, who at one point had an 0-for-22 streak. The media wondered if he was pressing. His response: "Pressing is just what people call it when you're not getting the job done."

DIANE WEISS

JULIAN H. GONZALEZ

Batting 1,000

Prince Fielder acknowledged the crowd's applause after he got his 1,000th career hit with a single in the first inning April 8 at Comerica Park. He finished with 182 hits for the Tigers in the regular season. Part of Fielder's success was that he didn't try to complicate the game of baseball.

"I try to make it as simple as possible," he said.

Toasted by teammates

Closer Jose Valverde doused teammate Prince Fielder during the champagne celebration on Oct. 1 in Kansas City after the Tigers clinched the American League Central title.

Fielder did his part that night, going 4-for-5 with a double and an RBI in the 6-3 victory over the Royals.

JULIAN H. GONZALEZ

the team

THANKS TO THEIR THREE STARS, THE TIGERS WERE PICKED TO DOMINATE THE AL CENTRAL BEFORE THE SEASON BEGAN. BUT MAKING THE PLAYOFFS WAS TRULY A TOTAL TEAM EFFORT, FROM ALEX AVILA TO DELMON YOUNG, FROM AL ALBURQUERQUE TO JOSE VALVERDE

ERIC SEALS

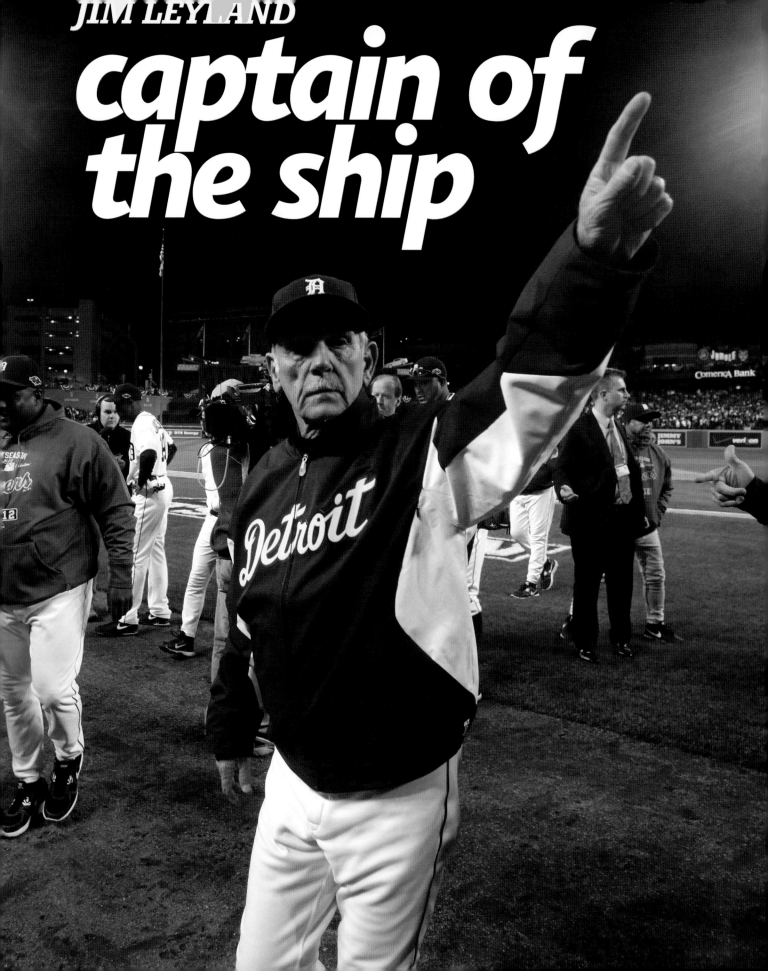

JIM LEYLAND
captain of
the ship

THE LEADER IN WINS AMONG ACTIVE MANAGERS OVERCAME SLUMPS, INJURIES AND SOME SURPRISINGLY TOUGH COMPETITION TO WIN A SECOND CONSECUTIVE AL CENTRAL TITLE

WILLIAM ARCHIE

KIRTHMON F. DOZIER

Next stop: Ohio

Jim Leyland, with Don Kelly, fielded plenty of questions about Victor Martinez's injury during the Tigers' winter caravan stop in Toledo. The manager kept his usual optimism: "We're going to be a good team. We're still a good team. With the team we have, even without Victor, if we pitch like I think we're capable of, we're going to be in the hunt."

Trophy ceremony

After the sweep of the Yankees was complete at Comerica Park, Jim Leyland got to hoist the American League Championship trophy, one that eluded the Tigers last season. Leyland battled his emotion and thanked the Comerica Park crowd. "We're one big happy family here," he croaked. "I'm just glad to be part of it."

Thank you, fans

Jim Leyland pointed to the stands after the Game 1 victory over Oakland in the division series. He appreciated the fans' support this season: "Sometimes I look around the stadium and I get a tear in my eye. I wish I didn't show it. But to see those people waving those towels? To see them so happy? I truly believe the game impacts their lives."

JULIAN H. GONZALEZ

JULIAN H. GONZALEZ

A friendly visit

Retired Cardinals manager Tony LaRussa paid his longtime friend, Jim Leyland, a visit during spring training in Lakeland, Fla. The two go back to LaRussa's days as the Chicago White Sox manager. Leyland was LaRussa's third-base coach in Chicago for four years.

Can't argue with success

Sure, Jim Leyland shared some choice words with the umpire crew in this May 1 game against Kansas City, but the outcome had to make him happy. With the 9-3 win that day, Leyland reached 1,600 career victories, 17th on the all-time managers list, passing Tommy Lasorda.

KIRTHMON F. DOZIER

Father-son moment

Jim Leyland and his son, Patrick, hugged after the Tigers' victory in Game 4 of the championship series over New York. "I believed all along — and it finally happened — that when you're a good club, at some point you're gonna play really good," the manager said.

DIANE WEISS

A NEW SWING ADDED A NEW DIMENSION TO THE DEFENSIVE WHIZ'S STELLAR LEADOFF GAME

JULIAN H. GONZALEZ

A changed man

Austin Jackson seemed to be known more for striking out than hitting in 2011. In 2012, hitting coach Lloyd McClendon called his leadoff hitter the new Austin Jackson. "If you compare last year and this year, it's definitely a big difference — I think that's what he (McClendon) means when he says that," Jackson said.

AUSTIN JACKSON
center stage

Playing the field

Austin Jackson made plenty of memorable catches this season, including this one on a fly by Raul Ibanez, who was the Yankees' best hitter in the postseason. Catcher Gerald Laird said: "Austin gets to balls that you don't see guys get to. And he gets to them with ease. He's had a couple of game-saving, pull-back home runs. A few times I'm like, 'God, I can't believe how high he can get sometimes.' "

MANDI WRIGHT

On the run

Austin Jackson chased down this long flyball for an out against the White Sox. "He takes pride in all facets of his game, " Brennan Boesch said of his close friend. "Guys think they've hit a double or a home run, and he catches it. He enjoys robbing hits from other people."

JULIAN H. GONZALEZ

JULIAN H. GONZALEZ

His bunting is no joke

Austin Jackson put down a sacrifice bunt, moving teammate Omar Infante to second base during Game 4 of the ALCS against New York. "You look at him when he plays — he plays the game so hard you think that he's such a serious guy," Tigers catcher Gerald Laird said of the centerfielder. "But behind closed doors, man, he's a funny guy."

Taking the lead

In the leadoff spot this season, Austin Jackson hit .300 with 29 doubles, 10 triples and a career-high 16 home runs among 163 hits. He drove in 66 runs. "He's settling down now to be the player we think he's going to be – and even better," manager Jim Leyland said.

KIRTHMON F. DOZIER

JOSE VALVERDE

papa grande style

JULIAN H. GONZALEZ

Hop, skip and a save

Jose Valverde made his usual moves coming out of the bullpen for Game 1 of the ALDS; he got the save after pitching a scoreless ninth against Oakland. The closer has always been known for his on-the-mound antics. "I enjoy the game so much. I like that all the fans like what I'm doing. So I dance."

CLOSER WAS FAR FROM PERFECT ... AND FAR FROM BORING

A good start

Jose Valverde got the save in Game 1 in the American League Division Series against Oakland. He pitched a scoreless ninth and struck out two in the 3-1 victory at Comerica Park. His pitching troubles started in his next appearance. "I have my confidence," the closer said. "I never lose my confidence."

JULIAN H. GONZALEZ

Playoff plummet

Jose Valverde didn't have the outstanding regular season like he did in 2011, when he was a perfect 49-for-49 in saves. But he did finish with 35 saves, out of 40 opportunities, in 71 games and an ERA of 3.78. Here, manager Jim Leyland gave Papa Grande a belly pat after the closer threw batting practice during a pre-World Series workout at Comerica Park. Media and fans alike wondered if Valverde would pitch for the Tigers again after he lost Game 4 of the ALDS and blew a four-run lead in Game 1 of the ALCS.

JULIAN H. GONZALEZ

Focused Fister

How does Doug Fister approach his opponents? "I'm going to take my best stuff and attack you with it," he said. "If that's what you are good at, and that's what I'm good at, we are going to go head-to-head, in a battle, and we are going to find out who is better."

JULIAN H. GONZALEZ

DOUG FISTER
master of command

AFTER AN INJURY-FILLED FIRST HALF, THE NO. 2 MAN IN THE ROTATION FOUND THE STRIKE ZONE, OVER AND OVER AND OVER AGAIN

Running strong

Doug Fister threw a shutout against Minnesota in September. Part of Fister's game preparation was running. He's somewhat of a running fanatic, having done half marathons in the off-season. At Comerica, he would "run poles," crossing the outfield, from one foul pole to the other, over and over.

DIANE WEISS

Cool customer

Doug Fister prepared for every game the same way, whether it was opening weekend or the World Series. "No matter what game you're pitching, it's important to stay focused," Fister said, "and to do the things you know how and the things you've done to prepare all year, whether it's been in the off-season or during the season, just to really kind of stay true to yourself and stay within your guidelines."

JULIAN H. GONZALEZ

Pumped for playoffs

In Game 2 of the World Series, Doug Fister became the first Tigers pitcher to make five straight postseason starts in which he went at least five innings and allowed two runs or fewer. He threw six scoreless innings despite getting hit in the head by a line drive in the second inning. "For me, it's a mind-set," Fister said. "You are not going to take me out of the game."

JULIAN H. GONZALEZ

DIANE WEISS

A delayed start

After two stays on the disabled list, Tigers right-hander Doug Fister finally got his first victory of the season on June 17. He strained his right side in his first start in 2012, and the Tigers couldn't find a successful replacement for him. He finished the regular season with a 10-10 record and a 3.45 ERA with 37 walks and 137 strikeouts. He also tossed two complete games.

A team player

Doug Fister had several discussions with catcher Gerald Laird during Game 1 of the ALCS vs. the Yankees. Fister held New York scoreless through 6 1/3 innings despite loading the bases in three different innings.

JULIAN H. GONZALEZ

MAX SCHERZER
the wild one

THE FIREBALLING RIGHTY STRUGGLED WITH HIS MECHANICS EARLY IN THE SEASON, BUT WHEN THEY CAME TOGETHER, HE WAS UNSTOPPABLE

MANDI WRIGHT

Bubble bursted

Twice in the playoffs, Max Scherzer was a victim of the no-rain rainout. It happened to him when he was scheduled to start in Texas in the 2011 ALCS and again in Game 4 of the 2012 ALCS against the Yankees in Detroit. He ended up getting the win vs. N.Y. the next day.

JULIAN H. GONZALEZ

Trading up

Since he arrived in the big 2009 off-season trade, Max Scherzer has made quite a name for himself with Detroit. Fellow pitcher Phil Coke said of him: "Max has done nothing but consistently improve each season I have seen him pitch as a teammate."

About face

The greatest triumph of pitching coach Jeff Jones' tenure in Detroit has been Max Scherzer. He has helped Scherzer develop into a feared starter, a pitcher who made a strong challenge to teammate Justin Verlander for the strikeout title.

JULIAN H. GONZALEZ

Strikeout streak

Max Scherzer struck out 231 batters in the regular season, 47 more K's than his previous career high of 184 in 2010. "When I'm able to execute the way I want to, strikeouts happen. It's a credit to how hard I'm working in between starts at fine-tuning each pitch," he said.

JULIAN H. GONZALEZ

JULIAN H. GONZALEZ

Smooth delivery

Max Scherzer finished 16-7 with a 3.74 ERA. "His pure determination seems to be something that's really driving him. He wants to be highly touted in the organization," teammate Phil Coke said.

Maximum effort

Tigers starter Max Scherzer would run through the empty stands at Comerica Park during off days in the summer. Scherzer, 28, just completed his fifth season in the big leagues, his third with Detroit. The right-hander was 43-27 in three seasons as a Tiger, with a 3.89 ERA.

JULIAN H. GONZALEZ

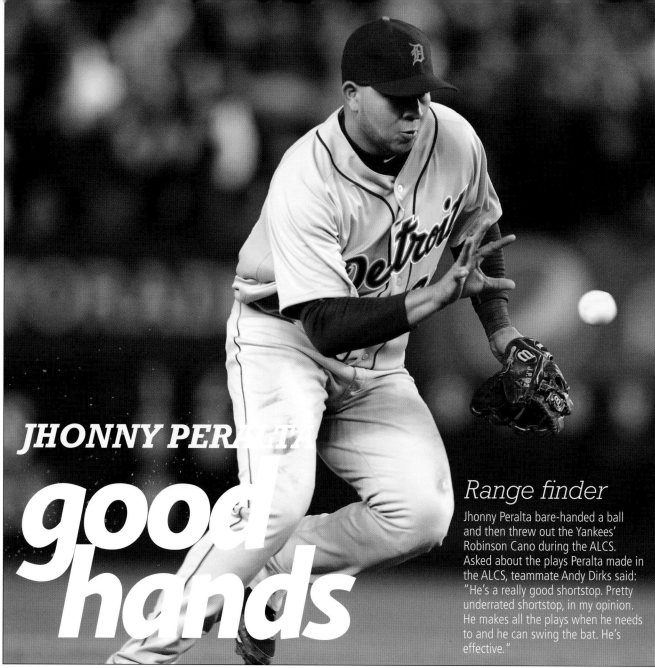

JHONNY PERALTA

good hands

Range finder

Jhonny Peralta bare-handed a ball and then threw out the Yankees' Robinson Cano during the ALCS. Asked about the plays Peralta made in the ALCS, teammate Andy Dirks said: "He's a really good shortstop. Pretty underrated shortstop, in my opinion. He makes all the plays when he needs to and he can swing the bat. He's effective."

JULIAN H. GONZALEZ

THE SHORTSTOP STRUGGLED AT THE PLATE, BUT SHINED ON DEFENSE

Double the fun

Tigers shortstop Jhonny Peralta played 150 games during the regular season, finishing with 63 RBIs and 32 doubles. He hit .239.

KIRTHMON F. DOZIER

ALEX AVILA *man of steel*

JULIAN H. GONZALEZ

Reason to smile

Alex Avila hit a double against the Athletics in Game 4 of the division series. The Tigers lost the game but came back to win the series in a decisive Game 5 in Oakland. "We learned through the course of the season that winning doesn't have to look pretty. And we certainly know that it isn't easy," he said.

Making the play

Tigers catcher Alex Avila made a diving catch against the Yankees in ALCS Game 3 at Comerica Park. Avila entered the 2012 playoffs healthy, a far cry from 2011 when he had a bad leg with fluid on his knee entering the playoffs and suffered through a rough postseason at the plate, hitting just .116. He injured his wrist in the 2012 World Series, though.

MANDI WRIGHT

call in the reserves

It seems every good team is good at picking each other up. The season is too long for just a few to carry the team. It's true of the 2012 Tigers. Some did much more than others, but almost everyone who played did something. Here is at least one standout performance per player that deserves to be remembered:

AL ALBURQUERQUE

On Sept. 29 at Minnesota, when a 6-0 lead slipped to 6-4, he got the final two outs of the eighth inning. The Tigers held on for the win that increased their lead on the White Sox to two games with four left.

ALEX AVILA

In the season's third game, April 8, with the Tigers losing by a run to the Red Sox in the 11th, Avila hit a two-run home run for the win.

DUANE BELOW

Doug Fister left the season's second game with an injury in the fourth inning. Below relieved him and didn't allow a run in his 2 1/3 innings for his first career win.

JOAQUIN BENOIT

On June 9-10 in Cincinnati, as the Tigers got the wins that began their climb from their season low to the World Series, Benoit guarded one-run leads with scoreless eighth innings.

JULIAN H. GONZALEZ

Welcome back, Dirks

After coming off the disabled list with a lingering Achilles injury, Andy Dirks hit the cover off the ball, batting .341 in his first 25 games.

QUINTIN BERRY

He pinch-ran against Toronto in the bottom of the 11th inning Aug. 23, and everyone knew he would try to steal. He did, and moments later he scored the winning run.

BRENNAN BOESCH

Boesch missed the playoffs, but so did the White Sox, in part because of Boesch's efforts. Each of his final three homers was a crucial piece in a win over the Sox.

MIGUEL CABRERA

In the third game — the game Avila won in the 11th — he hit a tying three-run homer in the ninth off Boston.

PHIL COKE

In the championship series, he got the biggest out when he fanned Raul Ibanez to end Game 3 and give the Tigers a 3-0 series lead.

ANDY DIRKS

His takeout slide at second Sept. 26 against Kansas City prevented an inning-ending double play and allowed the winning run to score.

OCTAVIO DOTEL

He replaced Jose Valverde after Valverde let a 4-0 lead get away in the ninth inning of Game 1 of the championship series. With all of Yankee Stadium ready for a victory by the home team, Dotel blanked New York for 1 1/3 innings, leading to the Tigers' 12-inning victory.

DARIN DOWNS

On Sept. 18, one day after the Tigers lost to the White Sox and fell three games out, Max Scherzer left after two innings against Oakland because of shoulder weakness. Downs relieved him and pitched 2 2/3 scoreless innings for the win. The victory began the 8-4 streak that carried the Tigers to the AL Central title.

PRINCE FIELDER

His two homers Aug. 17, one to create a tie, the other to break it, beat the resolute Orioles.

DOUG FISTER

Although he didn't get credit for the win, he set the foundation for a late September win over Kansas City when he struck out nine straight hitters, 10 total.

AVISAIL GARCIA

In the biggest play of the Tigers' season so far, the rookie rightfielder threw out Coco Crisp at the plate in Game 2 of the division series against Oakland. Without that play, the A's might well have won Game 2 and thus might have won the series in four games, before Justin Verlander had a chance to pitch the decisive Game 5.

OMAR INFANTE

His beautiful stop and glove-hand flip to second base preserved the Tigers' 1-0 lead in what became the clincher in Kansas City. They scored five runs in the next inning to take command.

BRANDON INGE

On April 16 in K.C., he hit his lone homer for the Tigers, a two-run shot that was the difference in Verlander's 3-2 win.

AUSTIN JACKSON

His running catch, amazing even by his standards, denied Toronto the go-ahead run on Aug. 23. The Tigers won in the 11th.

DON KELLY

He hit the ninth-inning sacrifice fly off strikeout artist Grant Balfour that beat Oakland in Game 2 of the division series.

GERALD LAIRD

On the night the Tigers had their first chance to clinch the Central, his three-run double in the sixth expanded their lead on Kansas City to 6-0. His hit became the difference in the 6-3 win.

JHONNY PERALTA

One night after his two errors admitted the winning run at Wrigley Field, his double was the big hit in a win over the Cubs on June 13.

RICK PORCELLO

On April 15, he prevented a White Sox sweep in Chicago by allowing one earned run in 7 2/3 innings.

RYAN RABURN

He hit one homer this season, but it was important. It was a three-run drive off Jake Peavy as the Tigers came back from a 6-0 deficit to win in Chicago in mid-May.

ANIBAL SANCHEZ

With his three-hit, 2-0 win over Kansas City on Sept. 25, he allowed the Tigers to catch the White Sox. The Tigers never fell out of first again.

RAMON SANTIAGO

With the Tigers a season-low six games below .500, he hit a solo homer in what became a one-run win at Cincinnati on June 9. This game marked the start of the Tigers' long climb toward the World Series.

OMIR SANTOS

The much-traveled catcher wasn't here long, but on June 2 his ninth-inning sacrifice fly drove in the winning run against the Yankees.

MAX SCHERZER

On Sept. 1, he beat the White Sox by blanking them for eight innings. He allowed four hits and struck out nine. The win was the difference between the Tigers moving within a game of the White Sox or falling three behind.

DREW SMYLY

In Yankee Stadium — where he stopped the Tigers' five-game losing streak with his first career win in April — the rookie left-hander beat the Yankees in Game 1 of the championship series with two scoreless innings in relief.

JACOB TURNER

With first place at stake July 22, he beat the White Sox for his first win. The next day, he was traded as the centerpiece of the deal that brought Sanchez and Infante.

JOSE VALVERDE

The Tigers' climb back from their season-low six games below .500 began in mid-June with a pair of one-run wins in Cincy. Valverde saved both in a hitters' park.

JUSTIN VERLANDER

After the Tigers got swept in a doubleheader by Minnesota with just under two weeks left in the season, he put them back on course the next night by going eight innings to beat K.C.

BRAYAN VILLARREAL

Those two wins Valverde saved in Cincinnati? Villarreal won both.

DANNY WORTH

On July 21 against the White Sox, a game with first at stake, Worth blooped a two-out hit in the fifth and scored the go-ahead run on Jackson's double.

DELMON YOUNG

After manager Jim Leyland had bemoaned the night before that the Tigers needed someone to hit the ball in the gap with a few runners on base, Young did just that to clear the bases in the seventh inning to break a tie and beat the White Sox on Aug. 31.

Praying to the playoff gods

With Jose Valverde's struggles in the ALCS, Phil Coke became an unlikely hero — and the closer — and the Tigers finished off the Yankees. "Unbelievable," pitching coach Jeff Jones said of his ALCS performance. "Cokey had an up-and-down year, as everybody knows. But he was there when we needed him."

MANDI WRIGHT

JULIAN H. GONZALEZ

One of the guys

Anibal Sanchez, far right, hung out in the outfield with fellow pitchers and catcher Gerald Laird before Game 3 of the ALCS. Sanchez came to the Tigers in a July trade that also brought Omar Infante to Detroit. "I just think he got to know the manager, the pitching coach, he got to know his teammates," Tigers manager Jim Leyland said of the progress Sanchez made late in the season.

JULIAN H. GONZALEZ

2012 TIGERS HITTING STATS

PLAYER	G	PA	AB	R	H	2B	3B	HR	RBI	SB	CS	BB	SO	BA	OBP	SLG
C Alex Avila	116	434	367	42	89	21	2	9	48	2	0	61	104	.243	.352	.384
UT Jeff Baker	15	37	35	1	7	2	0	0	4	0	0	2	10	.200	.243	.257
OF Quintin Berry	94	330	291	44	75	10	6	2	29	21	0	25	80	.258	.330	.354
RF Brennan Boesch	132	503	470	52	113	22	2	12	54	6	3	26	104	.240	.286	.372
3B Miguel Cabrera	161	697	622	109	205	40	0	44	139	4	1	66	98	.330	.393	.606
LF Andy Dirks	88	344	314	56	101	18	5	8	35	1	1	23	53	.322	.370	.487
DH Brad Eldred	5	17	16	1	3	1	1	0	1	0	0	1	6	.188	.235	.375
1B Prince Fielder	162	690	581	83	182	33	1	30	108	1	0	85	84	.313	.412	.528
RF Avisail Garcia	23	51	47	7	15	0	0	0	3	0	2	3	10	.319	.373	.319
C Bryan Holaday	6	13	12	3	3	1	0	0	0	0	0	0	2	.250	.250	.333
2B Omar Infante	64	241	226	27	58	7	5	4	20	7	2	9	23	.257	.283	.385
UT Brandon Inge	9	20	20	2	2	1	0	1	2	0	0	0	6	.100	.100	.300
CF Austin Jackson	137	617	543	103	163	29	10	16	66	12	9	67	134	.300	.377	.479
UT Don Kelly	75	127	113	14	21	2	1	1	7	2	0	14	22	.186	.276	.248
C Gerald Laird	63	191	174	24	49	8	1	2	11	0	0	14	21	.282	.337	.374
SS Jhonny Peralta	150	585	531	58	127	32	3	13	63	1	2	49	105	.239	.305	.384
2B Hernan Perez	2	2	2	1	1	0	0	0	0	0	0	0	0	.500	.500	.500
UT Ryan Raburn	66	222	205	14	35	14	0	1	12	1	1	13	53	.171	.226	.254
MI Ramon Santiago	93	259	228	19	47	7	1	2	17	1	0	20	39	.206	.283	.272
C Omir Santos	3	10	8	0	1	0	0	0	1	0	0	0	1	.125	.111	.125
OF Clete Thomas	3	0	0	1	0	0	0	0	0	0	0	0	0	0		
2B Danny Worth	43	90	74	9	16	3	0	0	3	0	0	13	23	.216	.330	.257
DH Delmon Young	151	608	574	54	153	27	1	18	74	0	2	20	112	.267	.296	.411
UT Matt Young	5	11	10	2	1	1	0	0	1	0	0	0	9	.100	.182	.200
Team Totals	162	6,119	5,476	726	1,467	279	39	163	698	59	23	511	1,103	.268	.335	.422

2012 TIGERS PITCHING STATS

PITCHER	W	L	W-L%	ERA	G	GS	CG	SV	IP	H	R	ER	HR	BB	SO	WHIP
RP Al Alburquerque	0	0		0.68	8	0	0	0	13.1	6	1	1	0	8	18	1.050
RP Duane Below	2	1	.667	3.88	27	1	0	0	46.1	49	25	20	6	8	29	1.230
RP Joaquin Benoit	5	3	.625	3.68	73	0	0	2	71.0	59	31	29	14	22	84	1.141
RP Collin Balester	2	0	1.000	6.50	11	0	0	0	18.0	14	14	13	5	11	12	1.389
RP Phil Coke	2	3	.400	4.00	66	0	0	1	54.0	71	28	24	5	18	51	1.648
SP Casey Crosby	1	1	.500	9.49	3	3	0	0	12.1	15	13	13	2	11	9	2.108
RP Octavio Dotel	5	3	.625	3.57	57	0	0	1	58.0	50	23	23	3	12	62	1.069
RP Darin Downs	2	1	.667	3.48	18	0	0	0	20.2	18	8	8	1	9	20	1.306
SP Doug Fister	10	10	.500	3.45	26	26	2	0	161.2	156	73	62	15	37	137	1.194
RP Luis Marte	1	0	1.000	2.82	13	0	0	0	22.1	19	7	7	4	9	19	1.254
RP Jose Ortega	0	0		3.38	2	0	0	0	2.2	3	1	1	1	1	4	1.500
SP Rick Porcello	10	12	.455	4.59	31	31	0	0	176.1	226	101	90	16	44	107	1.531
RP Luke Putkonen	0	2	.000	3.94	12	0	0	1	16.0	19	7	7	0	8	10	1.688
SP Anibal Sanchez	4	6	.400	3.74	12	12	1	0	74.2	81	36	31	8	15	57	1.286
SP Max Scherzer	16	7	.696	3.74	32	32	0	0	187.2	179	82	78	23	60	231	1.274
RP Daniel Schlereth	0	0		10.29	6	0	0	0	7.0	14	10	8	3	5	6	2.714
SP Drew Smyly	4	3	.571	3.99	23	18	0	0	99.1	93	49	44	12	33	94	1.268
SP Jacob Turner	1	1	.500	8.03	3	3	0	0	12.1	17	11	11	4	7	7	1.946
CL Jose Valverde	3	4	.429	3.78	71	0	0	35	69.0	59	34	29	3	27	48	1.246
SP Justin Verlander	17	8	.680	2.64	33	33	6	0	238.1	192	81	70	19	60	239	1.057
RP Brayan Villarreal	3	5	.375	2.63	50	0	0	0	54.2	38	20	16	3	28	66	1.207
RP Thad Weber	0	1	.000	9.00	2	0	0	0	4.0	10	4	4	0	2	1	3.000
RP Adam Wilk	0	3	.000	8.18	3	3	0	0	11.0	21	11	10	4	3	7	2.182
Team Totals	88	74	.543	3.77	162	162	9	40	1,430.2	1,409	670	596	151	438	1318	1.291

Big Al

Tigers reliever Al Alburquerque got the third out of the ninth inning in Game 4 against the Athletics in the division seres. Alburquerque was coming off elbow surgery last season and wasn't eligible to called up by the Tigers until early September. "It's like making a big trade acquisition to me," Tigers GM Dave Dombrowski said of getting Alburquerque back. He made just eight appearances in the regular season.

the year

162 GAMES OF EXCITEMENT PROVIDED ENOUGH MEMORIES FOR A LIFETIME

Maxed out

Prince Fielder clowned around with pitcher Max Scherzer, right, after the Tigers took a 4-2 lead in the seventh inning against the Pittsburgh Pirates on May 20 at Comerica Park. Scherzer became the second pitcher in the past 90 seasons to strike out at least 15 in seven innings, and the first Tiger to strike out 15 batters since Mickey Lolich in 1972. He also became the first pitcher since Astros right-hander Mike Scott on June 8, 1990, vs. the Reds to get all 15 strikeouts via a swing.

JULIAN H. GONZALEZ

JULIAN H. GONZALEZ

Historic moment

Doug Fister, after setting the American League record with nine consecutive strikeouts — touched the bill of his cap to acknowledge the crowd's applause as he left his historic game against Kansas City.

Fister of fury

Prince Fielder congratulated Doug Fister after the pitcher set an American League record with nine consecutive strikeouts against the Kansas City Royals on Sept. 27 at Comerica Park. Fister — who finished with 10 strikeouts — said it was a "special thing" to have teammates cheering for him. "It's a very humbling experience," he said. "I really couldn't put it into words. It doesn't change anything, but it's one of those things after the season is over, kind of look back and take a look at things. That's when I'll kind of re-evaluate and appreciate it."

JULIAN H. GONZALEZ

KIRTHMON F. DOZIER

So long, Inge

Brandon Inge's last game as a Tiger was April 24, a 7-4 loss to the Seattle Mariners. Inge was released by the Tigers on April 26. He was loved and despised by fans and was a veteran Tiger — he debuted with the team in 2001. "I know that for every one person that may boo, there are another 10 that are applauding," Inge said. "There's no reason to bad-mouth any of them. I'd rather be the bigger person and thank the people who are cheering than lump people into the negative category when that's not necessarily the case. Deep down, people are fans. They're not haters." He signed with the Oakland Athletics a few days later.

Hello, foe

Justin Verlander caught up with Oakland third baseman Brandon Inge before a game in Oakland on May 10. Facing his former team for the first time that night, Inge hit a grand slam in the eighth inning, but the Tigers won, 10-6. "I was kinda glad to get a fresh start, and I don't mean 'fresh start' by trying to get out of Detroit. I mean 'fresh start' by playing every day," he said. "I would've been very open to having a starting job in Detroit, too. That's home for me. That's family. But I knew that wasn't going to be the opportunity there. Getting an opportunity to start every day was key. That was the main goal."

KELLY L. COX/U.S. PRESSWIRE

SENDING EVERYONE HOME HAPPY

Eight of the Tigers' 50 regular-season wins at home came in their final at-bat. The list:

JULIAN H. GONZALEZ

Alex Avila hit a two-run home run in the 11th inning to give the Tigers a 13-12 victory over the Red Sox on April 8. The 4-hour, 45-minute game featured 25 runs and 35 hits. "One of the craziest games I've ever played," Avila said after he launched Mark Melancon's 2-2 curveball to rightfield. "I was running on fumes there. I felt like I caught like 350 pitches, five hours, however long the game was."

APRIL 5
TIGERS 3, RED SOX 2

After Jose Valverde blew a 2-0 lead in the top of the ninth, the Tigers strung together three hits and a hit batsman to push the winning run across on a single to left by Austin Jackson.

APRIL 8
TIGERS 13, RED SOX 12

Alex Avila's two-run home run in the 11th inning capped a wild game that saw the Tigers recover from a 10-7 deficit in the ninth inning and a 12-10 deficit entering the 11th inning.

MAY 4
TIGERS 5, WHITE SOX 4

Detroit trailed Chicago, 4-2, entering the eighth, before scoring once in the eighth (on a Miguel Cabrera single) and winning the game with a two-run home run by Jhonny Peralta.

JUNE 2
TIGERS 4, YANKEES 3

Another blown save by Jose Valverde became a win as third-string catcher Omir Santos lofted a sac fly to right to score Brennan Boesch with the bases loaded in the ninth.

JUNE 21
TIGERS 2, CARDINALS 1

Rookie Quintin Berry singled to center off St. Louis' Victor Marte with the bases loaded in the 10th inning to score Ramon Santiago. The single was Berry's lone hit in five at-bats.

AUG. 5
TIGERS 10, INDIANS 8

After trailing, 8-5, in the top of the 10th, the Tigers scored five runs with two outs off closer Chris Perez, including the final two on a homer by Cabrera that scored Omar Infante.

AUG. 23
TIGERS 3, BLUE JAYS 2

Berry, pinch-running for Delmon Young, stole second base with one out, then scored from second on Alex Avila's two-out single to rightfield off reliever Chad Jenkins in the 11th.

SEPT. 27
TIGERS 5, ROYALS 4

Avila grounded out with the bases loaded to drive in Don Kelly after Joaquin Benoit blew a start by Doug Fister in which he struck out nine straight Royals.

JULIAN H. GONZALEZ

Jumping for another series

DAYS OF ROAR
96

Ramon Santiago jumped into the arms of Quintin Berry after Berry's game-winning single in the 10th inning on June 21. The 2-1 victory over the St. Louis Cardinals clinched the Tigers' fourth straight series win.

JULIAN H. GONZALEZ

Many reasons to celebrate

The Tigers celebrated their AL Central title in Kansas City. It was a tough ride to the postseason. After being eight games back in the division on June 12, the Tigers went on two six-game winning streaks, July 4-13 and Aug. 1-7. "Winning never gets old," said Justin Verlander, "and we should celebrate this because this was a challenging season for us on so many levels, with all the stops and starts."

Miggy's magic

Miguel Cabrera's sixth-inning home run against Kansas City helped the Tigers clinch the American League Central title on Oct. 1 with two days to spare in the season. The Tigers had taken the division lead from the White Sox on Sept. 26. Sparked by his leadoff homer, the Tigers scored five runs in the inning. Cabrera went 4-for-5 in the game.

JULIAN H. GONZALEZ

STAYING GROUNDED

If you thought the Tigers work hard during the season, you should see the Comerica Park grounds crew. A typical day for the approximately 28 people who keep the field in shape rain or shine will last about 12 hours when the Tigers are in town. A look inside the work that kept Comerica Park a field of dreams all season long:

DIANE WEISS

The right conditions

Craig Skeltis spread infield conditioner over the infield skin near home plate before the start of a game and head groundskeeper Heather Nobozny smoothed it out. The clay conditioner absorbs and retains moisture.

DIANE WEISS

Rainy days

A downpour at Comerica Park brought out the grounds crew and a tarp.

DIANE WEISS

Stay within the lines

Stencils were a key tool for the grounds crew. An Old English D stencil is used on the pitching mound, while the frame in the background defines the batter's boxes.

First in place

Among the tasks of the grounds crew was inserting first base into its proper position.

DIANE WEISS

DIANE WEISS

Maintenance

Head groundskeeper Heather Nobozny helped water the infield clay before the start of a Tigers home game. The grounds crew formed a line to carry the hose around the field.

KIRTHMON F. DOZIER

Fans flock to stadium

Tigers mascot Paws got the crowd going before games. The average game attendance at Comerica Park was 37,383 in 2012, ninth among major league teams.

DAYS OF ROAR
100

KIRTHMON F. DOZIER

Sign of the times

The Tigers surpassed 3-million tickets sold in 2012 for the third time in their past six seasons.

DIANE WEISS

Fan appreciation

Tanner White posed with a giant Tigers ticket as he and his dad, Trevor White, were chosen as the Tigers' 3-millionth fan on Sept. 27. They also received a gift basket, a Miguel Cabrera autographed bat and season tickets for 2013.

THE TWEET TASTE OF VICTORY

Celebrities, sports media, fellow pro athletes, coaches and politicians — and even a presidential candidate — took to social media in October to congratulate the Tigers on their run to the World Series. Here's a sampling:

Mitt Romney (@mittromney): "Congrats to the Detroit Tigers on making it to the World Series! Part of the heart and soul of Detroit."

Michigan Gov. Rick Snyder (@onetoughnerd): "Congrats, Tigers! On to the World Series!"

Lions QB Matthew Stafford (@staff_9): "Congrats to the World Series bound Tigers! Very much deserved!"

Lions coach Jim Schwartz (@jschwartzlions): "Pumped about the @Tigers SWEEP of Yankees in ALCS. Skipper Jim Leyland has steered a steady course through rough seas all season. Congrats."

Legendary Lions running back Barry Sanders (@barrysanders): "I just want to say how proud I am of the @tigers WORLD SERIES BOUND! Maybe they will even have me out to a game."

Former Michigan Gov. Jennifer Granholm (@jengranholm): "Yes. Tigers sweep the Yankees! On to the World Series!!! Go Tigers."

Sen. Debbie Stabenow (@stabenow): "Wow! What a sweep for the Tigers. Now on to the World Series!"

Former Michigan hoops star and ESPN analyst Jalen Rose (@jalenrose): "We're going to the World Series Detroit! Go Tigers!"

Comedian Sinbad (@sinbadbad): "Congrats Detroit Tigers. You are going to the big dance. The city really needs this."

Donald J. Trump (@realdonaldtrump): "The Yankees are absolutely terrible — what happened to this team?"

MSU hockey coach Tom Anastos (@tomanastos): "Gotta love those Tigers!"

Lions DE Cliff Avril (@cliffavril): "Congrats to the Tigers going to the World Series…. #WIN"

Michigan musician Uncle Kracker (@unclekracker): "Congrats to the Detroit Tigers!!! They are unstoppable!!!!"

ESPN broadcaster Jemele Hill (@jemelehill): "We're going to the 'CHIP!!!"

Former Michigan hoops star and Piston Chris Webber (@realchriswebber): "BLESS YOU BOYS!"

Former UDM hoops coach and ESPN basketball commentator Dick Vitale (@dickieV): "Congrats to my buddies Jim Leyland & Gene Lamont & Tigers – SWEEP—WOW—YANKS BECAME A SOAP OPERA – Lot of changes coming!"

U.S. Rep. Hansen Clarke (@rephansenclarke): "Congrats to the Detroit Tigers. On to the World Series! Bring the championship back to the D!"

Michigan Attorney Gen. Bill Schuette (@schuetteonduty): "Brooms out. It's a sweep! Way to go."

Detroit City Council president Charles Pugh (@charles_pugh): "BLESS YOU BOYS!!! WE'RE OFF TO THE WORLD SERIES!!! GOOO TIGERS!!!"

Musician Alice Cooper (@realalicecooper): "GO @Tigers in the @MLB @WorldSeries! I'll be on my #NightOfFear tour in the UK, but I'll be watching at 1AM!"

Red Wings forward Cory Emmerton (@cemmer49): "@tigers are siiiiiiiiiick"

Home at first

Due to a new playoff format, the Tigers opened the playoffs at home against the Oakland Athletics despite being the lower-seeded team. They won all four of their home games in the ALCS and ALDS.

the playoffs

THE AL CENTRAL? CHECK.
THE ATHLETICS? CHECK.
THE YANKEES? CHECK.
THE WORLD SERIES? CHECK.

DIANE WEISS

STRIKING FIRST

JULIAN H. GONZALEZ

Seventh heaven

Tigers manager Jim Leyland greeted Justin Verlander after the pitcher finished throwing seven innings. Verlander allowed just three hits and one run while striking out 11 at Comerica Park.

Fast feet

The Tigers' Quintin Berry beat out an infield single that scored Omar Infante during the third inning. Oakland pitcher Jarrod Parker was changed with an error on the play.

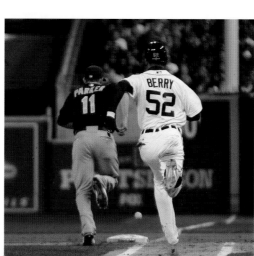

JULIAN H. GONZALEZ

The lone home run

Catcher Alex Avila hit the only home run in the fifth inning for the Tigers.

JULIAN H. GONZALEZ

9TH LIFE

MANDI WRIGHT

Game changer

Gerald Laird tagged out the speedy Coco Crisp at home plate during the third inning. Laird said if he had needed to move in either direction to catch the ball, he couldn't have tagged Crisp in time. "Coco Crisp is a burner who runs the bases well," Tigers pitcher Max Scherzer said. "The complexion of the game completely changes if he scores there. The game could have transpired so differently. The momentum came back on our side."

Not a crisp play

The Athletics' Coco Crisp was charged with a two-run error on Miguel Cabrera's bloop hit in the seventh inning that scored Austin Jackson and Omar Infante.

JULIAN H. GONZALEZ

Kelly's swing

Tigers Don Kelly and Prince Fielder, right, celebrated after Kelly hit the winning sacrifice fly to score Omar Infante in the ninth inning. Kelly was called up from Triple-A Toledo in September. "It makes it that much sweeter for DK to come through because he works his butt off, and he's probably the most positive teammate I've played with," Danny Worth said.

MANDI WRIGHT

Short-lived hope

Oakland's Josh Reddick celebrated his solo home run with Yoenis Cespedes during the eighth inning.

JULIAN H. GONZALEZ

JULIAN H. GONZALEZ

Long gone

Tigers centerfielder Austin Jackson could do nothing but watch the ball go over the fence off the bat of Seth Smith for a solo home run in the fifth inning. It was the first homer allowed by the Tigers' Anibal Sanchez since Smith had connected off him at Comerica Park three weeks earlier.

EXTRA CRISPY

JULIAN H. GONZALEZ

Downcast

Miguel Cabrera struck out during the sixth inning of the Tigers' Game 3 loss.

Robbed

The Athletics' Coco Crisp made a catch against the wall that robbed Prince Fielder of a home run during the second inning of the Tigers' 2-0 loss. "Coco's catch really got them into it," Tigers manager Jim Leyland said. "The key was they play deep. If he had played a normal centerfield, he probably wouldn't have got back to make the catch. It was a great catch."

JULIAN H. GONZALEZ

JULIAN H. GONZALEZ

Catch this!

After being robbed of two hits in Game 3, Tigers first baseman Prince Fielder led off the fourth inning of Game 4 by launching right-hander A.J. Griffin's 0-2 pitch far over the rightfield wall for a solo home run.

JULIAN H. GONZALEZ

Early departure

Max Scherzer left the game after 5 1/3 innings, allowing three hits and one run. The Tigers' right-hander struck out eight but got the no-decision after Jose Valverde gave up three runs in the ninth for the loss.

A tough test

Oakland's Coco Crisp is mobbed after hitting a walk-off RBI single. "This is baseball. This is why this is greatest game of all," Tigers manager Jim Leyland said. "You get tested all the time in this game. This is a good test. I thought we played our hearts out."

MELTDOWN

JULIAN H. GONZALEZ

ACED!

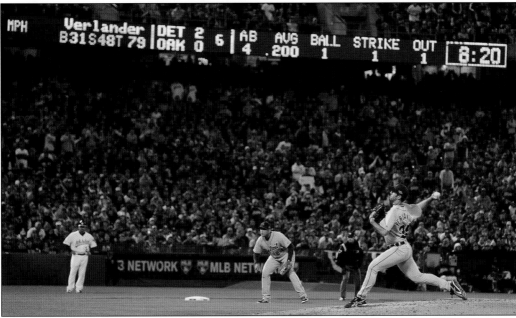

JULIAN H. GONZALEZ

Epic night

When asked to rank his Game 5 performance after the victory, Justin Verlander said, "I think this is No. 1. The two no-hitters are obviously up there, but that's something a little bit different. This is a win or go home. And I was able to go out there and have one of the better performances I've had."

Manager and Miggy

Tigers manager Jim Leyland got a hug from Miguel Cabrera after the victory. Cabrera was hit by a pitch in the seventh inning with the bases loaded to score Omar Infante.

JULIAN H. GONZALEZ

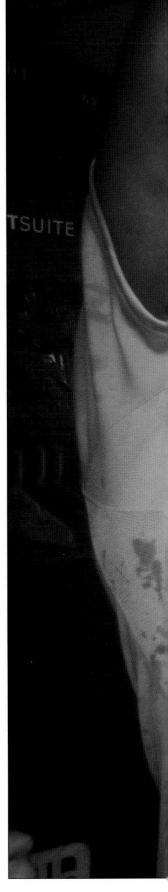

JULIAN H. GONZALEZ

Champagne, please

Jose Valverde, left, and Justin Verlander joined in the champagne celebration in Oakland after their series victory. "He had that look in his eyes … he was determined," manager Jim Leyland said of Verlander, who threw 122 pitches.

Delmon's dandy

In the eighth inning, designated hitter Delmon Young blasted a bases-empty home run. It marked his sixth postseason homer with the Tigers, the most in franchise history. Then in the 12th inning, Young's RBI double broke a 4-4 tie, scoring Miguel Cabrera. Young hit .353 in the series.

DIANE WEISS

A huge loss

Not only did the Yankees end up losing Game 1 at home after a four-run rally in the ninth inning, but they also lost their captain, Derek Jeter. He suffered a leg injury trying to make a diving stop and had to be helped off the field in the 12th inning. Jeter, from Kalamazoo, would go on to have season-ending surgery, and the Yankees would never recover in the series.

DIANE WEISS

Winning run

Miguel Cabrera crossed home plate, scoring the go-ahead run for the Tigers in the 12th inning at Yankee Stadium. The Tigers were able to bounce back after coughing up a 4-0 lead in the ninth. "We took a big punch," manager Jim Leyland said. "We took a right cross in the ninth inning but we survived it."

DIANE WEISS

ALCS: GAME 1
TIGERS 6, YANKEES 4 (12 INNINGS)

NEVER A DOUBT

JULIAN H. GONZALEZ

No way, Jose

Tigers closer Jose Valverde came in with a 4-0 lead in the bottom of the ninth and gave up two-run home runs to both Ichiro Suzuki and Raul Ibanez, making Detroit work overtime for its victory. His performance came on the heels of his blown save in Game 4 of the ALDS in Oakland.

JULIAN H. GONZALEZ

Arms race

Tigers starter Anibal Sanchez had the edge in days of rest, 4-3, over New York's Hiroki Kuroda and he ended up with the edge on the field as well. Sanchez pitched seven innings, giving up three hits and striking out seven. "Right now, I'm really, you know, together with the team," Sanchez said.

Second-guessing

The Tigers' Omar Infante was called safe on this play at second even though it looks like New York's Robinson Cano made the tag. Manager Joe Girardi argued the call and was ejected from a postseason game for the first time in his career. The Tigers would score two runs after that.

DIANE WEISS

Quite a catch

Alex Avila made a catch over the dugout on a ball hit by the Yankees' Mark Teixeira as Prince Fielder was ready to catch Avila. It was the third out of the eighth inning.

CANDY APPLE

JULIAN H. GONZALEZ

NO DEBATE

JULIAN H. GONZALEZ

Justin time

Starter Justin Verlander gave up just three hits in his 8 1/3 innings. His one run, and the Yankees' only run, came off a home run in the ninth. It was the seventh consecutive start won by the Tigers' ace. Through the first two playoff series, Verlander gave up just two runs total, both homers.

Young again

Delmon Young continued to make franchise history in the postseason with a home run off Yankees starter Phil Hughes in the fourth inning. The homer gave Young his seventh in the postseason as a Tiger. He was named the ALCS MVP. "As a child growing up, you always dream of winning Game 7 in the World Series with a walk-off hit," Young said. "So it's fun knowing that you're going there."

ERIC SEALS

JULIAN H. GONZALEZ

Coke and a smile

Phil Coke, who got the save in place of struggling closer Jose Valverde, celebrated after the victory. "We're firing on all cylinders," he said. "That's a very special thing to happen at this time of year." Coke became the first pitcher with two saves in the postseason after having one or no saves in the regular season while being used primarily as a relief pitcher.

JULIAN H. GONZALEZ

Pennant party

Max Scherzer, complete with his goggles, celebrated with his teammates at Comerica Park after the ALCS sweep of the Yankees. Scherzer had to wait almost 24 hours for his start — and his victory — after Game 4 was postponed until the next day because of bad weather.

KIRTHMON F. DOZIER

Brass for the brass

Manager Jim Leyland joined owner Mike Ilitch and general manager Dave Dombrowski for the championship series trophy presentation by honorary AL president Jackie Autry. Ilitch praised his players on the victory platform: "We don't have one hot dog in the bunch. ... They're humble and down to earth."

BROOM SERVICE

MANDI WRIGHT

Hello, World Series

Prince Fielder, left, and Justin Verlander celebrated after they completed their sweep of the Yankees to win the American League pennant.

Jubilation

The Tigers players ran onto the field in celebration after the final out of Game 4, finishing off their sweep of the Yankees. "You had the superstars — Justin Verlander, (Max) Scherzer, (Miguel) Cabrera and (Prince) Fielder – then you had the stories of Avisail Garcia coming up and getting big hits, of (Al) Alburquerque getting healthy and contributing, of (Don Kelly), of everyone doing something, " Alex Avila said of this team.

MANDI WRIGHT

BUMMER BY THE BAY

JULIAN H. GONZALEZ

Roughed up

Tigers starter Justin Verlander gave up five earned runs and six hits, including two home runs to Pablo Sandoval. It made for a rare short appearance for the 2011 AL Cy Young Award winner and MVP. He was pulled after four innings. "He really didn't pitch, obviously, the way he's capable of pitching," Jim Leyland said afterward. "He just didn't have a good game, and the Giants hitters did."

Panda-monium

Giants third baseman Pablo Sandoval, nicknamed "Kung Fu Panda," feasted on the Tigers' pitching in Game 1 and became one of just four players to hit three home runs in a single postseason game. He hit two off Justin Verlander and one off Al Alburquerque.

KIRTHMON F. DOZIER

DAYS OF ROAR
122

HEAD SHAKER

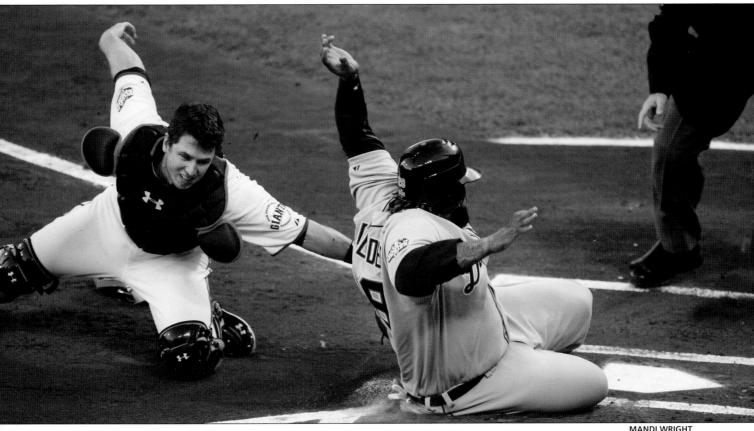

MANDI WRIGHT

Empty plate

Prince Fielder was out on this play at the plate in the second inning. Fielder took first after being hit by a pitch and tried to score on Delmon Young's double with no outs. But the throw from Marco Scutaro to catcher Buster Posey was right on the money. "They made a perfect relay. I was wrong," third-base coach Gene Lamont said. "If I had to do it over again, I can't say I would have sent him."

Headstrong

Tigers starter Doug Fister examined his hat after he was struck in the head by a line drive in the bottom of the second. He stayed in the game, becoming the first Tigers pitcher to make five straight postseason starts in which he went at least five innings and allowed two runs or fewer.

MANDI WRIGHT

JULIAN H. GONZALEZ

Foul play

It was that kind of day for the Tigers. Gregor Blanco's bunt stayed fair under the watchful eyes of home plate umpire Dan Iassogna and Tigers Miguel Cabrera and Gerald Laird. That loaded the bases for San Francisco, and the Giants scored their second run of the game as Brandon Crawford grounded into a double play.

DAYS OF ROAR
123

Collect 'em all

Stanley Maul of Allen Park wasn't planning on taking any swings with that bat. The giant bat was a promotional item Maul got signed by the 1968 and 1984 Tigers championship teams. He was at Game 3 working on collecting signatures from the 2012 team.

ROMAIN BLANQUART

Flood of fans

Ticket holders streamed into Comerica Park for Game 3 between the Tigers and the Giants. The announced crowd was 42,262. Detroit fans had plenty of confidence coming into the game since the Tigers had played so well at home all season and were 4-0 at Comerica in the playoffs so far.

MANDI WRIGHT

Behind the masks

Nick Morgan, left, and his brother, Alex, wore masks as part of their Game 3 garb at Comerica Park, but they couldn't mask their excitement about their favorite team.

ROMAIN BLANQUART

ERIC SEALS

Then and now

Joe Baker of Warren showed off his hat and buttons from the 1984 Tigers World Series championship as well as his ticket to this year's Game 3. Baker and his wife were outside Comerica taking in the atmosphere before heading in to watch the game on that Saturday night.

Outside view

On a chilly night in downtown Detroit, these fans were trying to stay warm — and hopeful — as they stood on East Adams outside Comerica Park to see the game.

ERIC SEALS

TRIPLE FROWN

KIRTHMON F. DOZIER

Lost opportunity

Miguel Cabrera put his head down after he popped out with two outs and the bases loaded in the fifth inning, closing the book on what would be the Tigers' last real scoring chance in another 2-0 game.

JULIAN H. GONZALEZ

One bad inning

Starter Anibal Sanchez pitched seven innings, striking out eight and giving up six hits. He was solid after a shaky second inning. His wild pitch put Hunter Pence on third with one out in the second. Then he gave up a triple to Gregor Blanco for one run. After Sanchez struck out Hector Sanchez, Brandon Crawford singled and centerfielder Austin Jackson bobbled it, leading to run No. 2.

OUT AT HOME

MANDI WRIGHT

Busted by Buster

Giants catcher Buster Posey, who won the NL batting title, hit a two-run shot to deep left, giving the Giants a 3-2 lead in the top of the sixth. It was his only home run of the series. "This is the ending you want to a good year," he said.

ERIC SEALS

Final strike

It was not a fitting end for Triple Crown winner Miguel Cabrera. He struck out, making the final out for the Tigers, who went cold at the plate. But pitcher Phil Coke was confident after the game: "I don't think there's a reason why you can't expect us to be here next year — on the other end."

DAYS OF ROAR
127

ERIC SEALS

Team players

Doug Fister was happy to hand over the American League championship trophy to teammate Miguel Cabrera during the on-field ceremony at Comerica Park after Game 4 of the ALCS. Fister started Game 1 of that series against New York, holding the Yankees scoreless, while Cabrera hit .313 with four RBIs against the Yankees.